HEALING THE SURVIVORS

8 STEPS TO WHOLE-SELF HEALING FOR
SEXUAL TRAUMA SURVIVORS

JACQUELYN WEIS

Cover Design: Michelle Young

Copyright © 2020 Jacquelyn Weis
All rights reserved.
ISBN: 978-1-950476-16-9

Note: This book references sexual abuse, depression, PTSD, self-harm and suicide. If a reader is suffering from any of these, this book should be used as a supplement to professional treatment.

This book is dedicated to the missing indigenous women and the families who have been affected and lost their loved ones.

INTRODUCTION

What if I told you that you aren't meant to live your life surrendering to your trauma? Would you believe me? We're often unable to see hope after trauma occurs. We quit fighting. We give up. We suffocate.

That's what happened for me. After my assault, my life came crashing down around me. I felt shattered, powerless, and broken. Everything I had been working toward in my life no longer mattered. It was like my entire life had been wiped away, cleared from all joy and happiness. I began to surrender to my trauma, and I allowed it to control the outcome of my life. I was left motionless, afraid, and suffering. I truly believed my life was over. Yet, there was this burning desire within me to push forward and reclaim my life because I...was meant for more.

And you are too.

During your healing journey, it may feel like you are broken and left crumbling into a million pieces. I've been there! I was at the breaking point of taking my own life. I wanted to give up, but there was something within pushing me to keep going. You may feel like you aren't in control of your life and

Introduction

that's okay. But as you heal and dig deep, you will find the strength and power to keep pushing forward just as I did. You are meant to heal and become a survivor! Allow yourself to move forward in your life so you can step into your full potential and a purpose driven life.

This journey taught me the whole-self healing approach to heal my mind, body, and spirit so that I could move forward in life toward my full potential. I started to unlock ways that helped me free myself from my trauma through energy healing, reprogramming, and a pursuit of a dream.

Once you begin healing, you will move toward the light and happiness you deserve. As you heal your mind, body, and spirit, they will connect you and assist you in finding and replacing the missing puzzle pieces in your life. They will bring you the inner peace that you need to move toward peace and light.

If you want to learn how to overcome your trauma and heal from within, you must allow yourself to connect, release, and transform. Something so simple can be exactly what saves you and transforms your life. You will start to awaken and find the tools that will help you rebuild and let go of the chains that are holding you back.

If you find yourself questioning, *How can I move forward and live another day?* Take your time to read this. I will connect you to the guide that saved my life and helped me heal and transform myself after my trauma. Let me be honest, it's not easy! There will be hard days! But as you take the steps to truly let go and heal yourself, you will begin to feel at peace and harmony just like I did.

Introduction

I want you to reflect on where you are right this moment. Are you at the beginning of your healing or in the middle? Where do you want to be? I want you to grab a journal. As you move through your healing, journal your thoughts throughout your journey. The things you write will become your inspirational story and will allow you to step into the fullest potential that you are meant to become.

I recommend taking this book one chapter at a time and making sure to spend time with the recommended exercises.

I am here. Let's go through this together. One step at a time.

STEP 1
FORGIVENESS

1
OVERCOMING SELF-BLAME

When we prepare for our healing journey, the first step is to allow forgiveness into our hearts.

I used to blame myself for my assault. I would think things like, *it's my fault, I shouldn't have gone to the party. I should have gone home when I had the chance.* The anger inside consumed me, launching me into a negative spiral trying to figure out what I did wrong or why someone would do this to me. Maybe you feel like me; maybe you are blaming yourself. I know how it feels, and I want you to know that it wasn't your fault.

We often blame ourselves for our trauma. We reflect and try to convince ourselves, *I deserved it. I asked for it.* It's real; it's raw. The guilt weighs heavily on us and often causes us to lose sleep at night trying to figure out what we did wrong. Why do we do that to ourselves? I've realized it's easier to blame ourselves than to think that someone could hurt us. By trying to solve unanswerable questions, it leaves us in more pain. We're left grasping to understand, desperate for a comforting answer to why someone would betray us. So, we end up with the conclusion, *it must have been my fault...*

During the first few months after my assault, I lived in a deep state of depression. At times, my greatest accomplishment was getting out of bed and washing my hair. I felt like a child. Weak, vulnerable, exposed. I was lost and didn't know what to do. When I tried to make sense of everything that happened, I completely fell apart. Dire thoughts consumed me, and I constantly blamed myself for what happened. I truly believed it was my fault, as though I did it to myself. My mind became a prison I was trapped within because I didn't know how to shut off my thoughts.

Our post-trauma instinct is to search for an answer. It's part of our body's fight or flight mode. Neither fight nor flight was successful, so what happened? Our mind races, replaying the scene nonstop to see if we missed something important that would somehow change our fate. We analyze every scenario: *What if I hadn't gone? What if I had stayed home? What if I wasn't alone?* Then the mirror blasts accusations again. *Maybe I was wearing the wrong clothes. I probably gave them the wrong impression. Maybe I didn't say, "NO!" loud enough.*

It's all a coping mechanism. All different versions of, *what could I have done to save myself from that situation?* Searching for a way to normalize our experience and make it okay.

A study by Duke University cited 62 percent of rape survivors blamed themselves for their attack[1]. Guilt and shame are common reactions survivors face. Because of the misconceptions about rape, we

Healing the Survivors

often blame ourselves, doubt our judgment, or wonder if we were responsible.

In some way, feeling like we are responsible and that it was our fault gives us a sense of control. When in reality, we weren't in control of that moment, and we have to accept that.

I spent a lot of time feeling that, but this is the truth: it didn't serve me well.

If we don't have control, we feel unsafe. Being unsafe means we will never be protected again. It changes us! We don't want to live in fear; we want to believe there is still hope.

When I was going through my healing journey of overcoming my sexual abuse, I was searching for ways to cope with my trauma. I was fourteen-years-old when the first time happened. I would constantly go back to the situation and find some type of loophole to put the blame on myself. It was like I was watching this never-ending horror movie. My uncontrollable thoughts constantly screamed, *it's your fault! You wanted it. You chose to go to the party.* The sad thing was...I believed it. The downward spiral led to me curling up in a ball and punching myself in the head. I absolutely hated myself, and I felt that I was the one to blame.

I share my experiences because I want you to learn from them—hopefully before you get to that point as well. What I did was damaging. One situation stripped my self-esteem, and I drowned my thoughts with self-inflicted habits as a result. These things only caused me more pain, and it ruined my relationships and friendships. I didn't know how to exist anymore, and I wanted it all to end.

When we start to normalize our trauma, self-blame takes over because we are trying to cope, but this often causes us more harm. We keep putting ourselves in that situation over and over again to try to undo the past. But what happened in the past can't be changed so analyzing this won't help you. It's time to shift your energy elsewhere.

When we try to cope with our trauma, we play mind games that don't end well. Our made-up reasoning for why everything happened allow us to believe we're finding closure when really it's the blaming of ourselves that holds us back from the healing.

As we heal, we have to be careful with who we are blaming in this situation—and if you're here, it's probably yourself. Allow yourself to let go of the blame.

> "In order to heal, we must first forgive...and sometimes the person we must forgive is ourselves."
>
> — MILA BRON

When you start to feel like everything that happened to you is your fault, I want you to journal about why you feel that way and what you would say to a friend if they were in your situation. Let those words of grace release you from your trauma.

Let me speak these very important words to you: You did nothing wrong! It wasn't your fault! I believe you! Please read these words over and over again. Now it's your turn to believe it.

Constantly remind yourself that this wasn't your fault, and your assaulter doesn't have power over you. **You have the power within to heal and move forward.** It all begins with the decision to do so.

∽

Repeat These Forgiveness Affirmations

I release negative, damaging patterns of thought and destruction to myself.

I approach myself with patience and understanding.

I love, embrace, and forgive myself of my past.

I uplift and reset my intentions to send myself love and positivity.

Today I commit to giving forgiveness the time it needs to blossom within me.

2

OVERCOMING ANGER

It's okay to be angry, and it's okay to be upset over what happened to you. It may feel like everything was stolen and ripped away, leaving you empty and broken. You may feel angry with the person who hurt you, angry for not being protected, and angry for being assaulted, manipulated, and abused.

I used to be so angry that I would end up screaming into the distance because I didn't understand why this happened to me. Maybe you feel this way right now. Own your anger. Just don't stay angry for too long because it will end up controlling your life.

Anger is a tricky emotion that we all feel. It's the way we process the trauma that we have faced. We often linger too long in this emotion, and it ends up causing us more pain and sorrow in the long run. When we are on a healing journey, we must truly heal at each step in order to move forward. Ask yourself, *what is holding me back from healing at this moment?* What is the emotion you are currently feeling in this moment? Maybe it's more than one, like hatred, anger, betrayal, forlorn, or bitterness. That was how I felt.

Did you know that hatred and anger are two of the most prevalent emotions that prevent us from truly healing? No matter who you're angry with—it could be the person that harmed you, it might be your family, or maybe yourself—if you don't take care of it, it will block you from the next steps.

When we are angry, it gives that person power over us. There would be moments when I was so angry, all I could do was curl up in a ball at night crying, screaming, and yelling! I wanted to punch something! I wanted him to know how I felt! I wanted him to know that he shattered my world, and that I was completely broken. Those reactions did more damage to me than to him. He will never understand what he did and how it could affect me for the rest of my life.

At fourteen-years-old, I turned to self-harm. The anger spurred so much hatred that, in an effort to cope, I drank, inflicted pain on myself, and entertained suicidal thoughts. I was desperate to escape. I wanted to die, and at times, I came close to taking my own life. It was awful, it was hard, and I know it weighed heavily on my relationships and family. It weighed heavily on me as well. I felt it every single day for almost a year! My life felt like it was crashing around me. I wanted to cry, I wanted to scream, I wanted to go and punch someone. I wanted to just let go of all the anger, but I didn't know how. I didn't know there was a right way, but I didn't want this person to have control over me, and I want to move forward.

It's a heartbreaking moment. It feels like we are

gasping for air just wanting someone to feel and hurt just like we do. We get stuck disintegrating, watching the pieces of our life fall apart. Instead, allow that anger within you to *move* you, not take your power away.

There was a breakthrough moment when I was tired of being angry and hurt. I didn't want to feel that way anymore. You probably don't want to be stuck like this either. I don't know where you're at on your healing journey, and I don't know if you're feeling exactly the way I felt or not. The suffering, depression, crippling post-traumatic stress disorder (PTSD). The sleepless nights of replaying the scene in your mind. Shutting down. Isolating yourself from other people. Scared to go out into the world. If any of this is familiar to you, this is why I want to help you continue through the next steps.

If you're ready to heal and you want to reclaim your power, you have to let go of the anger. When we are angry with that person, it blocks true healing from taking place. I was pissed off, I was hurt, and I felt unable to love or trust anyone. One day, I woke up and decided that I could no longer let my anger control me. I chose instead to allow my anger to push me forward. Oftentimes, our anger traps us from moving forward because it becomes a barrier between our happiness and us. When I decided to no longer be angry, I had to look within myself, forgive myself and allow myself to breathe through it.

I know it takes time, but one thing I realized was once I let go of my anger, that's when I started to see a shift within me. It allowed some of the bitterness to seep out. When we are searching for a way to cope, anger is the first thing that needs to be moved out of the way.

Did you know on a frequency scale, anger is the lowest vibration? The map of consciousness explains how emotions vibrate at a certain frequency. Frequencies affect your thoughts, health, emotions and belief systems. Nikola Tesla states, "If you want to find the secrets of the universe, think in terms of energy, frequency and vibration." So if you are in a low vibrational frequency there is where you will stay.

I want you to think about anger as a frequency. If you are constantly angry, you will stay angry and it will began to attract depression, shame, and guilt.

Our every thought, belief, emotion, and action as we consume on a daily basis creates the overall frequency of our bodies. This frequency is then sent out, like a radio tower, and brought back to you, like a boomerang.

Frequencies are energetic waves that stimulate our brain, which sends out frequency into our bodies. Whatever you consume affects you physically, mentally, and spiritually.

When you embark on the "healing" journey, especially on an energetic level, you are constantly releasing the lower vibrational frequencies that make up your baseline energetic frequency. As you release these energies it raises your vibrational energy. It will naturally attract positive experiences, like love, gratitude, joy, and peace, which all vibrate at the highest frequency. When you raise your vibration it helps your body get into alignment with what feels good and what you desire. When you are in alignment with these things, and the energies that were blocking you are no longer there, you are able to find freedom and clarity.

Anger attracts more pain. It attracts depression, anxiety, and heartache—even panic attacks. Once you decide you are done with the anger, you will release that anger and hatred inside of you. You are no longer angry with yourself or the world or the person. You will feel stronger because when you let go of anger, you will receive bits of your power again.

> "Anger is the inner child taking its power back. Anger is protection, self- defense, the awakening that you are a divine being of worth and value. Do not be ashamed about your anger. Honor it. Love it. Validate it. Use it constructively as fuel to dream bigger, love yourself harder, and accomplish your goals. Anger is the voice that says, "You deserve the very best."
>
> — SHAHIDA ARABI

We deserve to take our power and our strength back! We are bigger than that; we are powerful! Don't give them the advantage that takes away your power and your strength. Don't be angry—be disappointed, be sad. Those are okay to feel. Just let go of the anger because when you do, you'll feel that burning desire and the flicker of light inside of you that says, *yes, it's time. I'm ready to move forward.*

Affirmation Exercise

1. Use a pen/marker and write positive words all over your arm, hands, and face.
2. Stand in front of the mirror and read all the words out loud.
3. Take a picture and say these words every day for the next seven days.

3

FORGIVENESS WILL SET YOU FREE

As you step into forgiveness, you need to forgive yourself first. It's not your fault that this happened to you. I want you to think of forgiveness as this beautiful act that sets you free from your trauma. You can be your own hero. I know it will take time for you to reach this point, but when you are ready, seek the courage to forgive yourself and your abuser.

Forgiveness allows you to take more of your power back. It is the greatest gift you can give yourself as you heal. The abuser will not have control over you. When you forgive someone, you are no longer tied to that person. Forgiveness gives you control to take your life into your own hands to regain your strength and power. You aren't meant to stay stagnant. You are meant to thrive!

You have a choice in your healing to create a positive or negative outcome for where your life will head. You may feel stuck without a choice. By limiting yourself, you become a victim again. By forgiving, it no longer feeds the negativity beast. It helps you separate yourself from the negative outcome of your trauma. It's powerful. It can set you free.

I want you to visualize where you are right now in your journey. I would often describe it as feeling trapped in a cage waiting for someone else to see me, to open the door, to free me. What if the keys were in your hand the whole time? Would you unlock it, or would you wait for someone to let you out? Choose to set yourself free. You have the power to heal and change your life. You don't have to stay in the cage anymore.

"Forgive others, not because they deserve forgiveness, but because you deserve peace."

— Jonathan Lockwood Huie

Once I decided to forgive my abusers and myself, I felt such inner peace that it was overwhelming. I cried with joy. I felt in my heart that it was all going to be over. I was meant for greater things instead of being isolated in my room. I didn't want to be frozen in time unable to move forward. I wanted to have purpose, and I wanted to feel joy again. My entire body and spirit knew that I was going to get through this. I was ready to set myself free. I had a willingness to survive. I was determined to fight. I decided that day I was going to take the keys—my right to do so—and let myself out of the cage.

Allow yourself to take the keys. Let yourself out of the cage, and run toward your future. Gift yourself forgiveness. Do not let your trauma prevent you from living. Allow yourself to let go of all the pain, anger, and sadness! Keep healing because you don't want them to win. You aren't a victim. Use your inner strength to motivate you to heal and become your highest self. You are a survivor!

Forgive others and forgive yourself from any past situation, and you will be free!

Forgiveness Exercise

1. Write a forgiveness letter to yourself and to the abuser to set yourself free from the past.
2. After you are done, burn the letter.
3. Take a deep breath and get ready because it's time to start the next chapter in your life.

STEP 2
SPIRITUALITY

4

CREATOR/GOD/HIGHER POWER

In the midst of our trauma we often forget the most important piece to our healing. Whether you believe in a god, creator, higher power, or universal energy, we are still energetic beings experiencing something traumatic. During our healing journey, we are searching for *something* that will connect us to a greater purpose and bring us inner peace. When we are healing, we need spirituality because it connects the mind, body, and spirit together. Spirituality is the key to our healing. It is what creates connection, meaning, and purpose in life. When trauma takes place, we lose track of our purpose, we become blindsided by fear, and we lose hope and joy.

Our trauma causes us to separate ourselves from others and our surroundings. It leads us to believe we are alone and that we don't deserve love and support. We end up isolating ourselves. We get sucked into a dark hole of negativity and shame. The darkness envelops us, making us feel as though there is no way to escape.

> "Spiritual light will enlighten your mind and bring healing to your heart and joy to your days."
>
> — DETER F. UCHTDORF

In my Shoshone culture, we don't believe in separation between healing and connection to the creator. We believe they are all interconnected. You can't have one without the other. Allow this to bring you comfort. If you pray or meditate as you begin on your healing journey, it will bring you joy, happiness, and a calming energy. It will allow you to release your fear, depression, anxiety, and heartache on a deeper level.

In a study by The Mental Health Foundation, they found that people who prayed daily and meditated had a decrease in anxiety, depression, and PTSD[1]. The people who did not pray or meditate everyday had an increase of depression, suicidal thoughts, and feeling hopeless and lost.

At times, I could feel this negative energy creeping in on me. It began to influence my thoughts, my dreams, and my emotions. The darkness lingered amid my panic attacks. It always left me feeling powerless, drained, and ruined. The toxic energy would lead me into a downward spiral of self-abuse, surrendering to the dark force that sought my life. It was draining my light daily, and I didn't know how to escape it. What once was a burning fire within me was now a dim flicker of

Healing the Survivors

light growing weaker. The darkness grew stronger, taking over me physically, mentally, and spiritually.

If we lose sight of our spirituality it becomes harder to grasp onto positive light, especially when we go through something that shatters us and leaves us scrambling to pick up the pieces of what once was.

In my Native American culture, we are taught how negative energy disguises itself as something that is familiar. It takes form in many ways like our thoughts, emotions, memories, and fears. These things use our trauma against us to take us down and to take our power from within. If we allow our trauma to let us stray from our path to becoming our full potential, the disguised dark energy will convince us that we don't belong, that we are broken, alone, and guilty. It plays with our minds, inviting negative thoughts and removing the will to live. When we are healing, we must become aware of the separation of light and dark within our thoughts and emotions. Separating from the negative energies that are influencing and broadcasting abusive thoughts will allow us to regain our power and control.

I remember one night I had a dream. I was at a Native American ceremony, standing in the middle of a large circle. Medicine women clothed in white were walking toward me. Hundreds of them soon surrounded me, kneeling, praying. Three ladies speaking in Shoshone fanned me with an eagle feather fan. They were praying and casting out the negative energies in my body and casting out the dark energies surrounding me. They began to shield me. A woman draped a white blanket around me. They prayed for my protection and that my strength would return so I could heal myself and the spirit from my ancestors. As I woke up from this dream, I could feel this warmth that blanketed my entire body. That dream awoke something within me. I started to pray and meditate for protection and for the strength to heal myself. I was inspired to start casting out any negative thought that I had. I knew in my heart that my spirit was gentle and kind. I knew that it didn't speak ill things or spew the negativity that I had been battling for months. Over time, I started realizing that I had the power within to combat this mind game—and win.

Start to recognize your thoughts. If they aren't kind, command them to leave you. If you are having a panic attack, command that energy to leave you. Seize the power and strength behind every word you speak. Allow yourself to awaken your spiritual being. It will bring you comfort, and it will bring you strength. Actively bring light into your life each day. We aren't meant to stay in darkness. We are meant to rise out of the darkness and become a beacon of light. Awaken. Ask for strength. Ask for the power to stay in a positive state of mind and to be able to recognize these negative energies.

I challenge you to start listening to uplifting music, speaking kindly to yourself, and finding that inner strength to push through the darkness. Start to pray and connect back in with your spiritual self and the creator. You are powerful! You have the power to heal and fight. You are worthy of healing, and you are worthy of happiness. Start believing it today.

Repeat These Affirmations

I am powerful!

I am worthy of happiness and connection!

I allow my soul to guide me to peace and light.

5

SPIRITUAL DISCONNECTEDNESS

As we try to cope with our trauma, we can feel stuck trying to move forward. We feel off balance and disconnected. At times you may feel like you aren't truly present in your life. Your relationships might be falling apart right now. You may even be forcing yourself to get out of bed every morning. With every step to keep moving, emptiness still fills you inside. You are on autopilot. At this moment, you may feel like a zombie, moving through everyday motions, not truly living. If you are having anxiety or flashbacks, it probably feels like you are miles away from your present self. Yet there is something within telling you not to give up. Listen to it.

We are trying to grasp onto something real, yet it feels that our lives are slipping through our fingers. We ask ourselves if it's time to give up.

I have been right there too, on the verge of breaking, wanting to die, give up, pack up my bags and go home. It weighed heavily on me. I believed I was BROKEN. My panic attacks isolated me. I separated myself from connection.

Yet, quieting my thoughts long enough, I realized there was something in the distance calling out to me. My soul was pleading, "Don't give up yet, we just need a little more time." So, I went forward, still on autopilot, still empty, but listening to a faint calling.

I remember a dream I had during this period. I was sitting on my bed, staring off into the distance. My friend walked into my room and started speaking to me. Her voice was muffled and far away despite being inches away. Soon, she started to shake me, and I could faintly hear the words, "Jacquelyn, where are you?" When I was finally able to piece her words together, they echoed loudly in my head. *Where was I?* Once I awoke, I believed for a moment I was dead.

That's when I realized I was disconnected. Not just from people, but from everything.

When we face sudden or extreme trauma, we shift into the typical fight or flight response. When we aren't able to fight, we respond by flight. What happens if we can't physically flee? Our response is to disconnect spiritually instead. This is also known as dissociation. Researchers show that when sexual assault occurs, survivors go into freeze mode or they dissociate which means your brain shuts down or your mind "floats away," which can make you feel disconnected from your body. This is because your spirit and mind are trying to protect itself from the situation you feel trapped in. It's like a deer in the headlights external response, often resulting in feeling numb or vacant and emotionally detached within. After an attack has started, the freeze response can ramp up, taking utter control of a victim's mind and body. The brain actively "resets" itself, according to Jim Hopper, Ph.D., a clinical psychologist who specializes in victims' rights work[1]. This then leads to the survivor stuck in fight or flight mode post-trauma.

After the traumatic experience, it is normal for the body, mind and spirit to go into shock. Maybe you are like me, experiencing flashbacks or nightmares leading to the numbness. Allow yourself to reconnect and process the situation. I remember after the first time happened I was completely paralyzed. I disconnected, and it actually took three months after my assault occurred to fully remember what actually took place. Whatever your story is, you are not alone, and it's okay if you don't fully remember it, too.

Depending on what happened during your experience, you may have blacked out or felt a physical disconnection. Your body was trying to protect itself, but the response to disconnect leaves you unable to cope with your trauma and causes that lifeless and empty feeling. Now imagine trying to survive without your spirit connected to your body. That's what zombies are. Without your spirit, it becomes too hard to cope with sudden stress, trauma, and anxiety. Sometimes it's hard to connect to people or even the world around you. You're not fully present. The trauma controls you.

My trauma controlled my life for much too long. It prevented me from fully living, and the little living I did do was in fear. I was extremely disconnected with daily panic attacks. My breakdowns often led me to the floor shaking since every feeling was so intense. I couldn't think straight, I couldn't breathe.

It was terrifying. I would end up rocking myself to try to calm down. I wanted to escape that moment forever, and I truly believed I wouldn't survive it. Plus, there was always the looming anxiety, never knowing when the next nervous breakdown would hit.

Every time this happened, I could feel myself disconnect. I felt like my experience owned me, and I believed there was nothing I could do to change it. When our trauma thrives, it becomes hard to connect back to the body and to the world. But once we learn how to turn the autopilot off, we can take back control and feel once again.

That is when I started to learn about the spirit-body disconnection.

When the spirit experiences traumatic events physically and emotionally, it disconnects itself because it can't cope with the trauma. Our spirit cannot survive in darkness. It can only survive in light. When you are watching a horror movie and something scary happens, your automatic response is to close your eyes or, dependent on the level of trauma and its effects on you, turn the movie off. Our spirit responds in the same way. It needs to protect its purity. We cannot survive if we have a shattered spirit. Our spirit disconnection has a way of protecting us. If it stays fully present during trauma, we would not be able to handle the experience. We are divine beings not meant to suffer and stay in the depths of despair. When we connect the spirit to our body, it gives us the strength and power to withstand our experiences, and it leads us toward hope and light.

When I realized this, I started searching for a

way to connect. I wanted to regain my power. I remember the exact moment my spirit deemed it safe to return and when I became fully present. After I woke up from my dream, I walked into my mother's room. I told her that I felt disconnected and numb inside. She reached for sage and an eagle feather fan and calmly walked me outside. She had me stand barefoot in the grass, and we prayed together for almost an hour. Warmth and peacefulness washed over me. For the first time in a year, I felt joy and happiness. The small taste of it was all I needed to be ready to heal and feel safe to be present once again.

"Your sacred space is where you can find yourself over and over again."

— Joseph Campbell

When we connect to our spirit at its fullest capacity, we awaken the burning desire to survive and advance. The anxiety lessens and peace grows stronger. Allow your spirit to fully connect to your body. Let it support you and wrap you with comfort and love. You are worthy of connection; you no longer need to live in fear. Push forward and rise, you are powerful!

∽

Visual Exercise

Imagine light flowing around you. Take a deep breath and say the following out loud:

> *I am safe.*
> *I am powerful.*
> *I am strong.*

Take another deep breath, envision light flowing from the top of your head to your feet, and say out loud:

I connect my spirit to my body at one hundred percent where it belongs. I am safe and protected from all negative energies.

STEP 3
CONNECTION

6

CONNECTION WITH SOURCE

*A*s we take steps on our healing journey, we often get stuck unable to let go of the past. We search for an easy solution that will release us from our trauma, and often it doesn't happen from a one-step fix-all. Our trauma lingers, blocking us from living fully. Patterns of anxiety, depression, and fear prevent us from moving forward. At times we come close to destruction, sometimes even making rash decisions as a way to escape. Trauma leaves us grasping for air in a lifeless body that is just moving through the motions of existence but never feeling totally present. We think, *why am I alive? I give up. I can't do this anymore.* Yet look at you—you are still surviving and getting up everyday because there is something within you that isn't ready to quit.

There were many days when my worst thoughts won. I was trying not to give up, but everything within me resisted living. I needed a way to shut off and take a break from my current reality. I felt like I was living in the middle of a war zone called life. I started searching for the missing puzzle pieces to complete me, but no matter what I replaced that space with, it always left me feeling worse and even more depressed. I was trying to put a Band-Aid over my trauma instead of truly looking within and asking myself what was missing. I knew if I wanted to heal, I had to find the right puzzle pieces that had been lost, but I didn't know what they were yet.

When you begin to heal from your trauma, you need to elevate yourself to a higher consciousness. This will allow you to rid your body, mind, and spirit from the traumatic energies and emotions in your body that are causing you to re-experience your trauma daily. When you enter a space of elevation, it allows you to reconnect your spirit with your body. This connection will help you heal inwardly and slow down the chaos within you.

When I began searching for a way to calm the chaos within, I realized I needed to refuel from everything that had emptied me. I started praying to the creator, asking for guidance on how to heal and find the strength to move forward. One night, I went to bed with these profound questions at the forefront of my mind, pleading for help. That night, I had a dream that answered my questions.

In my dream, I was in a pitch-black forest and could barely see what was in front of me. As I walked through the forest, I could see a flicker of light in the distance. I slowly walked toward it. As I got closer, the sound of drums echoed in the night sky. The light transformed into a huge fire. I came to an opening in the forest, and the fire was in the center of the clearing. The drums played loudly but there was no one there. I could hear the whispering of my ancestors telling me to dance barefoot. I slipped my moccasins off my feet and started to dance. The earth pulsed underneath my feet. I felt alive, the energy from the ground moving through me. A bright light shined down on me; when I looked up, I could see the heavens opening. Dozens of eagles soared above me. I fell to my knees, and I began to cry. I felt all my pain shedding from me, and the darkness within me grew lighter. Suddenly, intense pain radiated from my back. It felt like something was tearing into me. I looked behind me to see enormous eagle wings attached to my back. I stood up, and I began to fly into the heavens, leaving behind the skeleton of my past.

When I awoke from my dream, I followed the haze of the dream and went outside barefoot. I stood in the grass and connected with the earth. The earth pulsed beneath my feet, and I felt the energy moving through me. Each breath I took brought a powerful vigor back into my body. I could feel the strength of the earth fueling my soul, and I knew this was a piece I was missing.

Once we start connecting to the earth and the natural energy around us, it refuels us with the right energy and connection we need to heal. It brings us might and power. This is called grounding, which will help regulate your triggers and anxiety. Grounding is a technique that uses the five senses (sound, touch, smell, taste, and sight) to help a person quickly re-orient to the present moment, assisting in managing anxiety, panic attacks, and more. Grounding allows you to awaken your senses and connect to the earth's surface, and that energy transmits into your body, which helps your body become present and relaxed. A study by Stephen T. Sinatra discovered that by using the grounding and earthing techniques, women and men who had extreme PTSD, anxiety, and depression experienced significant changes in their sleep and less negative symptoms[1].

You must connect with the source of all energy to begin healing. This will bring you a deep connection that your soul craves and will constantly feed your hunger for more.

> "A deep sense of love and belonging is an irreducible need of all people. We are biologically, cognitively, physically, and spiritually wired to love, to be loved, and to belong. When those needs are not met, we don't function as we were meant too. We break. We fall apart. We numb. We ache. We hurt others. We get sick."
>
> — Brene Brown

I challenge you to go outside barefoot every morning. Allow your body to release its negative energy and connect with the earth. Take deep breaths and imagine a light flowing from the top of your head down to your feet. Allow this light to go deep into the center of the earth and call it back to your body, allowing its power to center you. Take a deep breath as the energy fuels, gifting you power and strength to continue in your journey. As you restore your body, mind, and spirit, the source will continue to assist you in finding and replacing all the missing puzzle pieces. It will bring you the guidance that you need to move toward peace and light one step at a time.

∽

Grounding Exercise

Listen to my grounding meditations while sitting in nature or in a place of solitude every day.
https://anchor.fm/jacquelyn-weis

7

RAISE YOUR VIBRATION

The healing journey isn't always easy. If you have setbacks, don't give up. Keep your eyes on what's ahead.

I began having panic attacks daily as I worked to uncover the emotional turmoil from within. I had been healing myself, taking tiny steps to move forward, and then the unfathomable happened: I was raped for the second time. All my experiences resurfaced. My life crumbled to the ground once again. My fight for life briefly threatened to vanish, but then I realized I had the strength to pick myself up again. I did it once, I could do it again. I didn't want to go back to where I was before. That was no longer an option after everything I had discovered in the healing journey. So, I dusted myself off and searched for help to rise above it, focusing on my PTSD and panic attacks.

My mother took me to a Native Traditional Powwow. A powwow is a native ceremony where tribes from all around the world gather to heal and to connect back with the culture. We come together to honor our ancestors and to pray and dance. Each dance has a different cultural meaning, and there are some dances that are for healing.

As I stepped into the powwow arena, I was surrounded by the echoes and voices of our traditional songs. Dancers surrounded me, and I could feel their prayers giving me the strength and power to heal. I could feel the drums releasing my pain and heartache, and the voices of the singers brought healing into my heart and spirit. In that moment it felt like I was no longer shattered. It fueled me and helped get out of my mind. I felt elevated and I could finally breathe again. The vibration of the drums released the trapped energies in my body. I went home feeling calm and at peace. Weeks went by, and my panic attacks lessened. A shift happened within me that allowed the peace to flow through me once again.

The Native Traditional Powwow worked for me because it's my heritage. You need to listen to your soul's calling and what resonates with your innermost being.

As we begin to connect to our natural surroundings, we need to focus on the height of our vibrations. Everything in the universe is made of different frequencies, which affect how we feel, think, and manifest. When we vibrate at a higher frequency, we feel happier, lighter, and calmer. When we vibrate at a lower frequency, we feel depressed, angry, and heavy-hearted. Being energetic beings, we can attract the positive and negative outcomes in our lives. As we heal, we need to be careful of what we feed to our body, mind, and spirit because it affects us. Our thoughts, emotions, and vibrational energies attract positive and negative energies, experiences, and relationships. When we raise our vibration, we naturally elevate ourselves and are better able to withstand the negativity around and within us. Raising our vibration will allow us to awaken our subconscious. It helps us let go of suppressed emotions and energies that trigger us to feel anxiety, fear, depression, shame, etc. By raising the energetic vibration, it will allow you to live in a positive state of mind, and it will bring peace, power, love, joy, and clarity. See how much more power you have simply by choosing to do this?

A recent study by Dr. George Lindenfeld found that people who had PTSD, and listened to different sound frequencies at 100Hz had decreases in stress levels, anxiety, PTSD and significant sensory changes[1].

Since we are energetic beings, we gravitate toward light and darkness depending on the frequencies that are stored within us. Light attracts light, and darkness attracts darkness. If we stay in a lower frequency, we find ourselves in a depressed state of mind unable to cope with reality. When we begin raising our energetic frequency we begin to shift. It starts to get easier to cope with our trauma and emotions. We feel lighter and freer and more centered.

> "Your personal vibration or energy state is a blend of the contracted or expanded frequencies of your body emotions and thoughts at any given moment. The more you allow your soul to shine through you, the higher your personal vibration will be."
>
> — Penney Peirce

As you begin to meditate, allow yourself to vibrate higher. Allow your thoughts and energy to shift so that you will heal and overcome the traumas that you are facing.

Begin meditating to elevate the frequency in your body. Play sound bowl meditations, guided meditations, and diaphragmatic breathing techniques. Listen to classical music and surround yourself with things that raise your vibration. By doing these things, it helps us focus on raising the vibration in the body, mind, and spirit. It assists us in releasing stagnant energy preventing us from healing. These vibrations of the meditations restore balance and bring harmony within us.

∼

Journaling Exercise

1. What is your current reality?
2. What was lost because of this experience?

3. What do you need to change to allow yourself to elevate to a higher frequency?

Commit to these changes and continue meditating every day for thirty days.

8

EMPOWERMENT

What would you say if I told you that you have the power to heal yourself? That the power to overcome the trauma you have faced is within you? Would you believe me? It's okay if you don't. I didn't believe it at first either, but as I dug in deep and put intentional effort in searching for what I needed to heal, it got easier and the path started to unfold for me.

When we are on our healing path, it is easy to feel powerless and to allow our trauma to steer the wheel—the feeling that we can't survive or don't have the energy to keep existing. The helplessness. The one-step-forward, three-steps-back cycle. You are not alone in this.

I don't want you to think of your healing in a linear motion. Life is a circle, and your healing needs to mirror that. There are different stages in this circular path to your healing. In each stage, you are learning and growing, reclaiming your strength. In my Native American culture, we have a teaching called the Medicine Wheel. It teaches us of the stages of life and what we learn on our healing journey. At times, you may feel like you are an expert/elder, and other times you may feel like you are a child just learning and feeling vulnerable. We have to go through this process because it will deepen our healing so that we will be able to help others when we are ready.

When I began to search for the power within to bring me strength, I realized I had a choice because I already had the keys in my hand to take my power back. I didn't have to be a servant to my trauma anymore. I made a choice to no longer be a victim and that I would do everything I could to help heal myself. I wanted to be a true survivor. I let go of the victim mindset. I no longer blamed myself, the world, or the men. I didn't want to be tied to one moment in time, and I didn't want to be put in a box of shame, guilt, and despair. Once I let go of the label of being a victim, it all shifted for me. I felt the strength within to push forward.

We are deeper than our trauma. When we allow ourselves to realize that there is more to us than our trauma, we can feel more centered and peaceful. Think of your healing as never ending. Instead, healing brings a new life, like springtime after a cold winter. Thinking of it this way allows us to have hope for the future and what is in store for us. It will drive us to push forward in this new chapter in our lives, knowing that our story continues.

In my Shoshone culture, we believe that life encompasses the past, present, and future together. This allows us to heal as a whole to focus on today. Stay present in your healing, trusting the journey.

Search for your inner strength and consider your "why" to move forward. Ask yourself what your burning desire is for your life. Your answer will be a driver behind your empowerment. Meditate on it and realize that you are going to survive. You can and will heal from your trauma one step at a time.

When I began asking myself these questions, my "why" became stronger than the reason I should quit and end my life. It gave me power to fight even on the days my energy was low. I *chose* to heal from my trauma so that I could become someone else's hope. I wanted someone to know that it was possible to truly heal from our trauma and that it doesn't have to control us for the rest of our lives. Being motivated to become more pushed me to heal, releasing the negativity and darkness that surrounded me.

> "I am not what happened to me, I am what I choose to become."
>
> — CARL G. JUNG

Don't allow your trauma to control your life anymore. Choose to set yourself free and seek your "why." Find the reason why you are going to wake up every day and fight. Allow it to fuel your healing. Allow it to be bigger than the reasons why you can't move forward. Step into being a survivor and release the victim label. Your trauma no longer has control over you. Choose to move forward and allow yourself to transform.

Affirmation Exercise

I am worthy of healing.

I am a warrior.

I am releasing the negativity from within me and stepping into my fullest potential.

I have the power and strength to heal.

My why is _____.

This trauma no longer serves me.

STEP 4
INNER HEALING WORK

9
RELEASE TRAPPED EMOTIONS

What if I told you that you can release yourself from your memories and emotions of the past? Would you believe me? It took me a while to believe the concept, too. I grew up thinking it was safer to push my emotions to the side and try to hide them instead of acknowledging their existence. But let me tell you a secret that I learned. When we suppress our emotions and memories, it does us more harm than simply letting ourselves process the traumatic event and then releasing it from our body. I truly believe that you can heal and move forward by releasing your suppressed traumas.

Sometimes it can be challenging to tune in to what your body, mind, and spirit need to truly heal from the pain and trauma for good. We often suppress our experiences and file them away so that they no longer control us. We end up searching for ways to erase our memories and emotions so we can rid ourselves of the past. This can lead us to drugs, alcohol, self-harm, and addictions of all kinds to numb the pain inside. The memories never truly go away. They end up making us feel worse, and we fall into a deeper depression.

As I started searching for the missing pieces in my life, I kept trying to pull myself out of this depressed state. No matter what I did, it was only helping me learn to cope with my trauma, anxiety, and PTSD. At times, I felt helpless and ready to accept that I was going to be in this condition for the rest of my life. I believed I was going to be stuck having ups and downs forever because of my panic attacks. I was ready to truly step into my healing potential, but I struggled with how to do it. I was tired of being triggered randomly. I wanted to be able to go into the world feeling safe and not worrying about what danger may be lurking around every corner. I wanted my old life back. I wanted true freedom.

Going to therapy helped me lessen my anxiety, but it only taught me how to cope and not how to heal. I could feel there was still a massive block left by the trauma. Did you know the body stores trapped emotions and energies when trauma occurs? Learning about this was a game-changer for me. I could relate to it. I realized that during my trauma, I tried to protect myself from my experience, so I pushed the fear, panic, shock, and anxiety aside in desperation to simply survive. I never addressed them head-on. As time went on and the emotions multiplied and magnified, I continued to suppress my emotions and memories. Just like you, I wanted it all to disappear. By doing that, my body stored these emotions, which resulted in my panic attacks and depression. This was the answer I needed. I had to find a way to release these energies so that I could fully heal.

The more we deny and reject our emotions, the worse they get. Simple daily encounters can leave us feeling overwhelmed. It may feel like an elephant is sitting on your chest because of the pressure you feel from your anxiety. We often try to ignore it or are told to count the seconds hoping the feeling will disappear. But often it doesn't go away, and if it does, it doesn't last long before it reemerges. When we allow ourselves to feel and accept our true emotions, then the true healing begins.

As we suppress our emotions, our subconscious stores it so that we can release it once we are ready. Once I learned that there were ways to not only cope with my trauma, but to actually release it, I changed. I studied how emotions have different frequencies and how certain ones can cause the panic attacks and PTSD I was suffering from, all because of the ringing vibration in the body. Did you know that anger, shame, fear, guilt, depression, and self-abuse are the lowest frequencies on the consciousness scale of vibration? When our bodies experience these emotions, it sets off a warning and ends up triggering that fight or flight response. This leaves us stagnant and unable to cope with our emotions—stuck in a cycle where those emotions resurface every time they're triggered. Those emotions remain stuck in our energy fields and physical bodies resulting in stress, depression, panic, and low vibrational thought patterns, often leading to physical pain or illness.

JACQUELYN WEIS

> "When we release trapped energy and emotions, we raise the frequency in our body and energy field. This creates space for us to heal and elevate to a higher consciousness."
>
> — Dr. Bradley Nelson

Our emotions aren't meant to be in a constant state of being. They are meant to come and go. Imagine what life would be like if you no longer had these emotions trapped in your body. You would feel lighter, you would be able to breathe, your anxiety would disappear, and you would no longer have panic attacks.

Before I was introduced to *The Emotion Code* by Dr. Bradley Nelson, I suffered from extreme anxiety. I didn't know that I could actually release my suppressed emotions. When my mother's friend, Tracy, introduced me to *The Emotion Code* method, I had no idea what to expect other than the fact that I was ready to try anything that might help. When she started the process, I was amazed that I didn't have to relive my experiences, nor did I have to talk about them. Tracy began releasing emotions from me one-by-one. Fear, shock, panic, helplessness, self-abuse —the list went on, and as she spoke about each one and nailed the age that it occurred, all I could do was nod in agreement and awe of the accuracy. My subconscious knew which emotions were ready to be released, and the experience allowed each one to surface and release in a very safe and positive way.

Healing the Survivors

At the end of my session, I felt lighter; the heaviness I carried for years lifted. Tears filled my eyes, and I began to cry because I finally felt free and happy.

Honestly, I expected the anxiety to come back immediately after the session. I had carried it for so long. Days went by, then weeks, then a month, and it never came back! I was forever changed from one session, and it's what launched me on the track to becoming an Emotion Code practitioner as well.

The Emotion Code has assisted people with PTSD, anxiety, and depression. Many people have reported feeling happier, lighter, and optimistic after releasing trapped emotions. I recommend that you look into *The Emotion Code*. It will change your life forever. There are practitioners ready to help you move forward and heal. Check out my website (www.JacquelynWeis.com) to schedule a session!

Allowing the subconscious mind to release the root of our trauma will allow healing to take place. Choose to no longer allow your trauma to block you from becoming your full potential self. Step forward and allow your subconscious to awaken and guide you through your healing.

∼

How to Release Trapped Emotions from Your Body

1. Think about a specific age when trauma occurred.

2. Write down the emotions you felt during that event.

3. Imagine light flowing from the top of your head to your feet. Say, "I release _____ (negative emotion) completely from my body, mind, and spirit."

4. Take a deep breath!

5. Write down positive emotions you want to replace these negative emotions with.

6. Say, "I replace this negative emotion with _____ (positive emotion)."

10

RELEASE MEMORIES

One of the cruelest parts about trauma are the memories that we are left with. They are often more traumatic than the actual experience because we unwillingly relive them over and over again. Our memories become distorted based off what we recall and what we piece together, resulting in a more traumatic memory of our experience, which leads us to PTSD. After a while, we struggle to determine the difference between reality and our memories. The two merge together leaving us in constant fear because we don't know how to discern the difference, and we begin to doubt ourselves. We try to suppress our memories to protect ourselves because they are too overwhelming to comprehend spiritually, physically, mentally, and emotionally. This often results in us feeling immobile because as much as we wish it weren't confusing, we also don't want to remember the entire reality of it. Every place, situation, sound, scent, scene, and event put us at risk of a panic attack or flashback. We become traumatized and try to make the experience go away, but it ends up controlling us every day.

These events leave an imprint on us that lasts. I remember days when I just wanted to forget life. I wanted to shut off my memories and make them disappear. I remember praying to the creator to just make it all go away. I remember days when seeing a park would trigger a flashback, or a smell would trigger me and send me into a spiral. Some days I would completely shut down and wake up curled up in a ball screaming. Our minds become stuck in an ongoing memory match game leaving us in a constant panic and scramble to explain ourselves or make the next move. Maybe you have felt like me, or maybe you are currently going through this. Despite the struggle, let me tell you there is still hope.

Through my healing journey, I discovered that we can reprogram our memories so that we are no longer triggered or left re-experiencing our trauma on a daily basis. I experienced a painless way to let go and rid myself of these memories through *The Body Code* by Dr. Bradley Nelson and through Neuro-Linguistic Programming. It taught me that we can uproot the negative memories and transition them into a positive memory that results in a neutral state about the memory—this is more positive overall. These steps allow us to reprogram our brain so it no longer searches to activate the negative memories again.

Researchers have shown that traumatic memories constantly intrude into the consciousness. They proved that when we recall a memory, it impairs our brain and causes us to relive the experience over again allowing our body to respond in fight or flight. This alertness causes stress symptoms that further

Healing the Survivors

intensify the memory, making it hard to depict what is real and what actually occurred.

If you are ready to let your memories go, make sure to read this next part carefully. Your memories aren't meant to control you. Allow them to surface and release peacefully from you. You aren't doing this alone. I am here to help you.

"Until you let go of the painful memories of the past in your life you will not be able to learn and grow. The beauty of life is to learn and grow, the day you let go of your past you will continue to grow. Let it go and restart your life."

— CHARLES E. HUDSON

As I began releasing my memories through the process, I found that my memories no longer triggered me. I no longer felt tied to the experience, and I could move through it easier if I thought about it. Instead of feeling negative emotions like anxiety, panic, and fear, I felt peace, happiness, and neutral emotions, focusing on the survival more than the traumatic event itself. I felt free from my experience and like I could actually move forward in my life.

Your memories no longer have to control you. Allow yourself to learn about a new solution as I did. It could be the one that finally frees you so you can step into your fullest potential.

How to Release Traumatic Memories

1. Think about a positive experience.

2. Say, "I am safe, and I am supported."

3. Write down the positive emotions you feel when you think of this experience.

4. Take a deep breath!

5. Go into that negative experience. What emotions are you feeling?

6. Take a deep breath and say, "I release these negative emotions."

7. Replace these emotions with a positive saying, "I replace this emotions with _____ (positive emotion)."

8. Say out loud, "I release this memory completely from my mind, body, and spirit."

9. Revisit the positive memory.

10. Drink water.

11

RELEASE CORDING

If you have followed the other chapters so far, healing from our trauma can be done quicker and easier now. We are able to rid ourselves of our trauma, and we are able to let go of the past that is preventing us from stepping into our full potential. But we can't just release our memories and emotions and be done. There is one last piece that we are missing that will fully allow us to move forward. This last piece is called an energy cord.

Did you know that we can create energy cords with other people? And that they allow us to absorb energy from each other? It is natural to create energetic cords with others, but it's when it turns into a negative energy transaction that it needs to be released. It's like an energetic umbilical cord that is created during trauma, which often leaves us connected with our abuser. Cording is the energetic result of an overwhelming situation due to trauma. When we experience the body feeling overwhelmed and shocked by an assault that you are unable to process, it leaves the cord lingering unresolved. All forms of sexual assault or violation leave a scar deep within us. It often results in carrying the offender's energy with us until it is removed. We could end up living our entire lives with these cords because we had no idea they existed, and we were never educated on these energetic imbalances that were created.

I soon discovered that I needed the release of an energetic connection. It made sense. At times, I felt like there was something attached to me, like a rope from my past holding me back from moving forward in my life. That's when the energy cord connection came into play.

When I was introduced to energy cordings, I didn't know that it could leave such an impact on my life. I found out that because of this cord, I was absorbing my abuser's shame, guilt, negative energy, and more. I learned that the reason I blamed myself was because that energy was transferred to me.

As I sat on the couch next to my mother, her friend helped me release these energetic cords. I sat in complete stillness while she worked. Like the emotional healing session, I still had doubts that it could be successful, that it could be such a simple process. But I was willing to do whatever I could for healing.

Earlier that morning, I could hardly get out of bed. I hated that it was a struggle and that I wasn't in control over my life. Then Tracy started her work in releasing three energy cords attaching me to other people. She had me imagine standing in front of each person and cutting the cord off that was connected from the outside of my body to theirs. I visualized the process one-by-one. Tears ran down my cheeks, but I wasn't feeling sadness. I felt...freedom.

I felt like this enormous weight was lifted off my chest and that I could breathe for the first time. I cried because I no longer had to be connected to those people. I could move forward.

Once you release these negative energetic connections with your abuser, your power becomes yours. The freedom you will feel once you are able to release it is life changing. For me, weeks, months, even years went by when I didn't have PTSD and panic attacks. Releasing these cords was the turning point in my healing journey. I had full control over my mind, body, and spirit. Your inner peace will grow when you free yourself and no longer allow another person or trauma to control your life.

I recommend not doing this alone. Seek a Body Code Practitioner for help or schedule a session with me to help release this cord. If you are choosing to release this on your own, here is how. You can also check out my podcast on cord cutting meditation at www.anchor.fm/jacquelyn-weis.

By cutting these cords, it will set you free. Allow yourself to take back your power, strength, and energy. They no longer have control over you. You are…FREE.

∽

How to Release Energetic Cords

1. Envision light surrounding you and covering you from the top of your head to your feet.

2. Say, "I am safe and protected."

3. Imagine the abuser in front of you.

4. Imagine an umbilical cord attached to you and your abuser.

5. Take a deep breath and envision cutting the cord off with a weapon or light energy.

6. Say, "I release this cording completely. It no longer serves me, and I release you and me from these binds. This cord is destroyed and never to return again."

7. Imagine light flowing into your body and replacing the empty space in your body where the cord once was.

8. Say, "I recover all energy back into my body. My energy flows back into me and creates a peaceful energetic boundary of love and light."

9. Listen to a sound bowl meditation or go for a walk after.

10. Drink lots of water for the next twenty-four hours.

STEP 5
CONSCIOUS HEALING

12

RELEASE NEGATIVE PROGRAMMING

As we go further in our healing journey, we have to make sure to heal our behaviors and negative mindset as well. During our trauma, we developed a survival mindset based on our experience due to living in daily fight or flight mode. We needed to be able to make quick decisions and act quickly. This makes it hard to think clearly about the future and to stay positive on a daily basis. We are stuck with a mindset that no longer serves us. We must fully rid ourselves of the thinking patterns that left us spiraling into self-abuse, anxiety, and panic. These patterns caused us to overthink and overanalyze everything we came into contact with. It allows the results of the trauma continue to control the way we think, breathe, and function.

I understand why we do this and trust me, it took a while to get out of it, so I don't expect this to be an easy step. But at this point in our journey, we can no longer allow our mindset to block us from moving forward. We can't survive with belief systems and behavioral patterns that leave us stuck in a victim mindset. As we transition, we must let go of these negative beliefs, thoughts, and behavioral patterns. But how do we shift from a negative behavioral pattern to a positive behavioral pattern to help us heal and move forward?

By now, much of your healing should have progressed. But if you are still getting stressed or triggered and dealing with it through self-abusive behaviors, avoiding reality, or through negative coping patterns, you should be aware that these behaviors often worsen your mental and physical health. The constant stress and anxiety are forced on your body, mind, and spirit. Developing negative behavioral patterns leaves us unable to cope with reality and drained emotionally, mentally, and physically. Plus, it blocks us from thinking clearly and adapting to high intensity situations.

Our reactions to events that trigger stress, panic attacks, flashbacks, traumatic memories, and emotions time and again often lead us to isolate ourselves. We feel ashamed, different, and sometimes like no one will understand us. Sometimes we even think we need to guard our family and friends from our problems. As we remove ourselves from social situations, our depression grows stronger. We feel like we are alone, which multiplies the negative thoughts and anxiety. Did you know that by surrounding yourself with a support group, it will not only empower you, but it is actually needed to heal from and cope with your trauma?

I remember when I finally decided to tell my family a year after I was raped what had happened. The support and love I received from my family and community was something I could have used in the beginning, and I wished I hadn't waited so long.

Healing the Survivors

They empowered me, and the burden I was carrying alone had been lifted from me and shouldered by others. In my Native American culture, we are told that whenever someone is in pain or grieving, we grieve together. That person isn't meant to do it alone, and we are encouraged to hold space for that person so they can truly heal.

Why did I wait so long? It would have been so much easier if I had just told someone. I realized I caused myself more pain and suffering by not telling those who loved me what was going on. Instead, I let my ego win and told myself, "I have to do this alone." We aren't meant to do this alone. We need a support system. If you don't have one, I invite you to reach out and join the "Healing the Survivors" private Facebook group. Please don't carry this alone anymore. The first step toward a healthier approach to prevent future negative behaviors is reaching out for support.

To understand our negative behavioral pattern, we have to know what it looks like. When we are trying to cope, our mind turns those patterns into blueprints for survival, but often it causes us more harm. For example, you may have developed a behavior of pretending everything is okay. This may leave you constantly creating different realities for yourself, making it difficult to stay present within your own life. You become stuck looking to escape, which leaves you depending on unhealthy social events in desperation to not be alone with your own thoughts. Or you may have developed the behavior of overanalyzing your trauma. This may leave you constantly feeling exhausted and anxious, so you end up locking yourself away in your room because of how intense your thoughts are. Whichever behavioral patterns you have developed, know it doesn't have to last forever. You can still change them.

Survival mode is an automatic response, but it's not a healthy one to be in. I was constantly living in fear, depression, and anxiousness and was mentally blocked as a result. It wasn't until I started going to therapy that I realized that I was also blocking myself from fully living my life because of my mindset. At that moment in time, I was in a cycle of labeling myself as a victim. My mind provided a way to escape, but it was actually crippling me from my future. I chose the path of isolation and no longer went to school because I couldn't cope with society. I had convinced myself that I couldn't handle daily situations and that the only way to handle my anxiety was to completely remove myself. My body and mind could no longer function with my anxiety and stress, and they started shutting down. I was completely burned out. I was constantly stressed and exhausted and unmotivated to move and survive.

I especially recall one night when I got stuck in a downward spiral of negative self-talk. I couldn't do anything, and my adrenaline was pumping quickly. I wanted to escape it, but I didn't know how. I battled this for hours and by the time the clock struck one o'clock in the morning, I was spent. I didn't know what else to do anymore, so I put my shoes on and I ran. I ran twelve miles that night. What was I running from?

Healing the Survivors

"What consumes your mind, controls your life."

— Todd Cahill

Don't allow your thoughts to control the outcome of your life. It is time to change the pattern so our bodies no longer live in a reactive state of mind.

Our bodies react to negative emotions and thoughts the same way it does to seeing a bear. Adrenaline becomes a driver. Our brain and nervous system work in overdrive, which causes us to feel burned out. The exhaustion comes from our body and mind constantly running from something with no end in sight.

When we analyze something, our brain rapidly tries to upload and download every piece of information about our experience so that it can give us the best result. But when we face trauma and are stuck with that pattern of adrenaline rushing at us constantly, we get stuck making quick decisions. We are left unable to process what is real and what is not, so we end up with the victim mindset—our brain keeps telling us to "fight" or "run" as if being chased by that bear. In that moment I was in with rapid-fire negativity my body screamed, "RUN!" and it believed there was no way out but to flee.

We aren't meant to stay reactive and on edge all the time. Our body needs time to relax and recharge. To change the pattern of constant reaction, we must acknowledge the old behavioral patterns and transition them into a positive pattern. As we begin to understand our day-to-day and step-by-step processes of our thinking patterns that tend to slip into the abusive thought patterns, we will be able to catch ourselves quicker to transition our thoughts and behaviors so that we can change them. If you find yourself going down the negative self-talk hole, remind yourself you aren't a victim. Remind yourself that you are a survivor, and you are strong and powerful. Say it as many times as necessary until your thoughts begin to settle with the truth of your strength. Allow yourself the peace that follows so you can enter a relaxation state and thereby move forward in your life in a positive way.

∽

Shift from Surviving to Thriving

- Become aware of your emotions and triggers.
- Analyze how you respond to different sounds, images, and words.
- Have a plan. Write down your step-by-step process that works for you to calm down in the midst of chaos.
- Find a creative outlet.
- Connect with the earth and find a support system.

13

INSTALL POSITIVE PROGRAMMING

We can no longer live life by reacting. Our bodies and mind will burn out and become exhausted. We must dig deep and heal our patterns so we can move toward happiness and freedom.

As I began to heal my mindset, I was able to pull back enough to analyze each of my behaviors and thoughts. I noted the behaviors that constantly left me battling my recovery process. Even though I believed I was deserving of healing, the negative thoughts in my brain were subconsciously telling me that I should give up and that I wasn't worthy. I had developed a mindset of survival, and the resulting behaviors often left me alone and introverted. Harmful thoughts of *I hate myself*, *I am a failure*, and *I will never be loved* took turns rotating in my mind. No matter what I did, I couldn't escape them. These statements would leave me depressed and motionless. I truly believed every word. I accepted it as my fate.

The way we think and process determines our

future. Our thoughts can cause us to stay stationary in our lives, which will prevent us from healing and moving forward. We aren't meant to be stagnant. We are meant to rise and thrive. We can no longer allow the way we perceive ourselves to jeopardize our future.

In the beginning, it may feel like our thoughts are telling us truths. But let me tell you, our mindset is based on our emotions, and if we continue to feel angry, depressed, or sad and abuse ourselves, we will always live in thoughts that bring us down each day.

"To realize that you are not your thoughts is when you begin to awaken spiritually."

— Eckhart Tolle

Realizing how much our thoughts control the outcome of our lives allows a shift to take place. Oftentimes, we get stuck in the negative thought patterns and forget to reflect on and consider the truth.

Sometimes your thoughts are going to take you down. Other days they will uplift and motivate you to keep moving forward. Whenever I battled my mindset, I would only give myself ten seconds or less to consider a negative thought. I would ask myself, *is this a true statement or emotion-fueled?* It turned out to always be false. Don't let these lies convince you that you aren't worthy of love, happiness, joy, and success. You are worthy! You deserve the world more than anyone else! Now believe it!

When trying to change your mindset, feed yourself positivity every day. Create daily affirmations that you repeat to yourself in the morning and that you can easily recall if you start to slip into a downward spiral. Catch yourself in the moment of any self-abusive thoughts and quickly shift to positive ones instead. Begin to look at life with a silver lining. Find something to keep you motivated to keep pushing forward. For me, my silver lining was, well… you. I knew that if I could heal myself and get out of this pit that I was stuck in, I would be able to help others do the same. I want to thank you. If it weren't for you, I wouldn't be here writing this to help you heal. So, decide what you are going to live for and allow that reason to push you daily.

Once we are able to remove our negative mindset, we are better able to create positive behaviors and thoughts that will allow us to think in positive ways. Choose to improve your feature by seizing more control over the thoughts that enter your mind. Fear, worry, and panic distort our energy, which causes us to lose sight of what is real. Your thoughts from here on out will determine your daily actions that will pave the way to healing and unlocking your fullest potential.

∼

Affirmations to Change Your Current Mindset

Stand in front of a mirror and say out loud:

I love you, I accept you, and I honor you.

I am worthy of forgiving and loving myself at my fullest capacity.

I am strong and can withstand anything.

14

ASK FOR HELP

As you develop a new mindset and new behavioral patterns you will begin to think more clearly, and it will give you hope and purpose. It will motivate you to move and feed the fire that is burning within you. It is time to write a new chapter of your life that will propel you forward and bring you peace, love, and joy. The question you need to ask yourself is, *what do you want your new path to look like?* This will determine the steps you take. Allow yourself to dream and think of your future in a positive way. Don't allow yourself to become stagnant. Your life is in your own hands. It's time to dust yourself off and rise! You are meant for greatness, so allow yourself to seek a positive future. What is it going to be?

When I allowed myself to envision what my future was going to look like, it was hard at first to imagine a life without depression, anxiety, and PTSD. But the idea of it gave me hope. It gave me a reason to fight for my life because I didn't want it to end in my current state. I knew deep down I was meant for great things. I was tired of blaming myself, and these men stripped away my happiness and ripped away my self-worth for far too long. So, I gave myself permission to dream and then I put that dream into action.

I started by imagining myself in a life where I was successful, happy, in love, and stepping into my full potential. I focused on the image of me in love with myself, radiating and standing confidently. The more I thought about it, the more real it felt. With that as my focal point, I organically shifted and transformed into the exact person I wanted to become. There were hard days, of course. Some when I felt more fake than authentic and wanted to give up. But when those hard days came, my goals and dreams are what got me out of bed and kept me driven.

What does this future you look like? Who is it that you want to become? What are the reasons you're driven to heal? You are allowed to rid yourself of your past and finally move forward. Allow yourself to propel forward and reach your goals. Grant yourself grace along the way for the hard days and celebrate the good days. Be patient with yourself and maintain an encouraging mindset. You have the power within yourself to rewrite your story, and you are the only person who can change it. Sometimes the easiest way to change your future is by changing your perception of how you want things to be in your future. Become okay with your current reality and allow yourself to move on with your life.

You have the power to choose this right now. You can decide to move on with your life at any time. You are deserving of a life that thrives. Accept yourself and heal yourself so that you can truly move forward. Get rid of any negative self-talk and negativity that fuels you. You can heal from this and have an incredible life! But you must make the decision to do it.

∼

Journaling Exercise

What is your current reality? What needs to change?

What is your "why" for healing and moving forward?

Who does this person look like?

Who do you want to become?

STEP 6
FINDING INNER PEACE

15

RAISING YOUR VIBRATION

What is blocking you from having inner peace? Does it feel like peace is something that you haven't unlocked the door to? As you begin to heal, you will start unlocking the doors that will lead to you finding your inner peace. Oftentimes we feel like we don't have access to it, that it's something we have to earn, and we begin to question if it will ever come our way. Have you given up on the idea that there is a heaven within your hell?

Inner peace once seemed out of reach because my emotions and ego controlled how I reacted. Some days it felt like I was just a passenger along for a drive while my ego navigated everything that came into my path, and my emotions went into overdrive. How exhausting is it to operate like that, though? Feeling like I was constantly under pressure waiting for something else to go wrong, the anxiety a constant undercurrent.

> "Inner Peace begins the moment you choose not to allow another person or event to control your emotions."
>
> — PEMA CHODRON

We can feel blocked from receiving peace and sometimes it will be difficult to reach due to the power of our emotions. We may begin to feel that we aren't worthy of anything serene. Maybe you might feel like you aren't good enough to rise to a higher level.

One thing I learned was that inner peace comes from inside you. I know it sounds obvious with the "inner" descriptor, yet inside of us is one of the last places we search. You can't find inner peace elsewhere. We turn to other people or things to provide that peace for us because it's too hard to believe that that is something we can provide ourselves.

Without consciously being aware at the time, my search for inner peace led me to look for something or someone outside of myself to fulfill this hole inside. I began to depend on the relationships I was in because I didn't believe I could make myself happy. I became codependent on my relationships to provide me with fulfillment. I grew to hate being alone because the emptiness would ring louder, which led to breakdowns because I was terrified to do life alone. I didn't know how to provide for myself the happiness I craved.

Once you start searching for your inner peace, you must search for it within yourself and nowhere

Healing the Survivors

else. You do not need someone or something else to provide it for you. It might seem easier said than done at this moment, but trust me, the longer you wait to realize this, the harder it will become to find it within. I caused more pain to myself by being so dependent on others for my happiness and peace. Sometimes it might feel like you have to dig deep to find that strength to trust yourself, but once you remove the blocks that no longer serve you, you will discover your inner power and light that provides you with everything you need.

Allow yourself to pull out that peace from within. Seek your own strength and power because that is what creates your joy and happiness. I want you to close your eyes and imagine walking through a miraculous garden filled with blossoming flowers and vibrant colors. As you walk through this garden, you notice you are breathing with ease. Every scent is heavenly and pure. Your entire body feels peaceful and centered. You see a huge fountain in front of you, so you walk toward it. You stop and stare into the water and notice your reflection. As you stare at yourself, you are filled with love, joy, and happiness. The words "I am free" come to you. You inhale and slowly exhale and feel the power and strength rise from within. Suddenly, you can see your future, and you're excited for what is to come. Now open your eyes and take a deep breath, and hopefully you can feel the stirring in your soul.

When we get to this point of our healing journey, we may find ourselves longing for the day we can feel centered and at peace with ourselves and our lives. We pray for the morning when we wake up full of gratitude and joy with each breath that we take. We hope that soon this is how we will start to experience life.

I yearned for peace and joy every single day. I would constantly imagine this garden so I could escape and feel centered just for a short moment in time. The short moments slowly became longer moments with each practice of this exercise.

We have to let go of the judgment of our past and allow ourselves to love and accept who we truly are. We can no longer have false images of ourselves as we heal. We have to love ourselves unconditionally and find peace with the past. It is no longer in your control. But your emotions and thoughts are within your control, and choosing positive ones will allow you to stay more centered and discover more peace each day.

~

Affirmations

I am worthy of love, happiness, and peace.

I am grateful for _____.

I am worthy of receiving inner peace each day.

I am in control of my emotions, and I am in charge of the outcome of my day.

16

SELF-LOVE

As we begin to press forward to become greater than our trauma, we must be kind and gentle to ourselves along the way. Often we are too critical toward ourselves that we forget about what we have overcome. This leads us to putting ourselves down with abusive thoughts.

One thing I learned during my healing was that as we move forward, it is important that we feed ourselves regular doses of positivity and love each day. If we remain judgmental, we constantly block ourselves from moving forward.

You want to avoid falling into the hole of judging and criticizing yourself each day. When you do this, your body and mind automatically react with each abusive word you think, speak, joke, or whisper. It will affect your mood and cause any chaos that remains within to arise.

Let me be honest, self-love isn't easy, especially after sexual trauma. It was something I had to make a conscious effort to do. But we need that positivity and love because without it we will never fully heal, damaging ourselves again with each negative word spoken.

Self-love is the key to healing and freeing ourselves from our trauma. Why? Because when we can love and accept ourselves, it will give us the strength to believe there is hope in a better tomorrow.

I want you to know that you are worthy of loving yourself and of receiving love. If this is hard for you to believe, please keep working on the ability to own this about yourself. I remember after I was raped, I believed that I was broken and unworthy of receiving love. I was so damaged that I even believed that love didn't exist at all, so why would I ever bother loving myself? I was ashamed of my trauma and hated myself for it. There would be days where I would abuse my body because of my despair and revulsion. But the more I hated myself, the deeper into a depression I fell. It didn't matter what my boyfriend would say, nor did it matter what my family or friends would say. I had closed the door on love, and the only way that door would be opened was if I truly loved and accepted myself again.

I know there are days where we are extra hard on ourselves, but imagine if there were more days of being embraced? What might have you experienced if you accepted yourself more?

I remember when I started challenging myself to look in the mirror every morning and say out loud, "I love you, you are amazing, and you are good enough." At first it brought me to tears. I avoided looking myself in the eyes to get the words out. I felt vulnerable, uncomfortable, and unworthy of such a statement. I realized that if I couldn't accept love from myself, how was I going to be able to accept it

Healing the Survivors

from others? I needed to love myself first before believing someone else could love me, and that required a change to be made.

Now imagine, how would you feel if you told yourself that every day? *I love you. You are amazing. You are good enough.* How would it change you? Would you finally start believing it? Once you start to embrace yourself, it will help you let go of any negativity that has a hold on you. When you fully love yourself, it will help you withstand your trauma. You will feel empowered to take bolder strides to continue moving forward in your life.

When I started my self-love journey, I made the commitment to wake up and meditate and then stand in front of the mirror. I would feed myself loving thoughts and affirmations. Every day that I did this, I would feel lighter and happier. I felt more receptive to my own love and love from others as well. My thoughts became less critical, and I noticed that even my anxiety and depression levels lowered.

"To fall in love with yourself is the first secret to happiness."

— ROBERT MORLEY

When you decide to make the conscious effort every day to feed yourself love and positivity, you will notice a shift in your energy level, thoughts, and perception of yourself. Self-love is one of the most powerful gifts you can possibly give yourself. You are worthy of love and of receiving it. I challenge you for the next thirty days to be mindful of how you treat yourself. Feed yourself more loving thoughts. It will completely transform you.

∼

Self-Love Challenge

Every day for the next thirty days, stand in front of a mirror.

Name five things that you love about yourself physically.

Name five things that you love about your personality.

Say "I love you" five times.

17

SPEAKING OUT

"When we deny our stories, they define us. When we own our stories, we get to write a brave new ending."

— Brené Brown

I used to be ashamed of my story. I hated everything about it because it made me struggle to accept myself. It caused a lot of heartache for many years. My story wasn't something I wanted to own. I didn't want it to be true, and it was easier to pretend it didn't exist than to accept that it happened to me. I didn't want to be another statistic for Native American women. Nor did I want it to trigger my whole generational line. But I knew deep down if I didn't own it and if I didn't heal from it, my trauma would be passed down energetically.

In my culture, we believe in historical trauma. Historical trauma is trauma that has not been dealt with adequately in one generation, so it gets passed down energetically, carried through our DNA, in our behaviors and in our thought systems. If the trauma doesn't get released, it will continue to be passed down to future generations. Because of this, I knew that I had to own my story so that I could heal myself and the generations to come. My trauma is greater than just me. I worried that it would be my fault if it happened to someone else. On a deeper spiritual level, I knew I had to heal this energetically, and I had to speak out against rape because I couldn't expect someone else to do it for me.

Once I owned my story, I began realizing that I had a choice on how my story played out. I got to choose what my truth was and how the story ended for me. I didn't have to be the victim anymore! I didn't want to focus on the trauma because it didn't deserve to have control over the rest of my story. I wanted my story to define me in ways of resilience and strength, and that comes from rising above our circumstances.

Choosing to focus on the valleys of our story can cause us to have negative perspectives on our lives. Declaring ourselves victims, for example, can cause us to feel powerless and destroyed, allowing the abuse to reign with power. However, declaring ourselves as survivors means that we reclaim our power and we're granted freedom. So, choose to be a survivor! It will set you free from your trauma, and it will help you find peace within your own story. You are allowed to rewrite your story and create a new ending. You can change the story from something so traumatic to something that created purpose and a beacon of light to someone else. There is a powerful force that arrives when we own our story. It allows us to accept our whole selves.

When I finally owned my story, I felt empowered. I decided that I would write the end of my story in a positive light. I allowed my story to move me forward instead of holding me back. I chose to keep the trauma in the past. Once I said that I was done with it, it released me, and the heaviness melted away.

As you start to own your story, allow yourself to rewrite the ending you desire. Allow yourself to accept your whole truth and find peace that has given you a new perspective to help others. You are a survivor, and you are strong! When you don't feed into the pain anymore and you decide what you want your outcome to be, you have more room to manifest the life you desire.

Don't be silent anymore. Speak out and share your story with others. Take back your voice and become the voice for others. Own your story and take your power back. You are worthy of it!

Always remember that your story is yours. You don't have to tell it to the world. You don't have to tell it again and again. Share your story only when and where it feels right for you to do so. Your story is powerful, and you are resilient, so allow yourself to choose how to use your power.

∽

Journal Entries

What is your truth?

How has this affected your life?

Are you ready to move forward? Why?

How are you empowering yourself moving forward?

What is your survivor story?

STEP 7
REBIRTHING

18

SPIRITUAL TRANSFORMATION

As we awaken our inner selves, we will begin to transform from the inside out. Our trauma will no longer hinder our path because we have simply changed our fate. As we strive to heal, we have to create balance in all aspects of our lives. It is a key component to having a balanced life because if one area grows weak, it will cause us a great deal of pain.

Our spirit, mind, and body can no longer work separately. We must allow ourselves to connect these together. We cannot allow this separation to exist, and if we do, we will feel lost completely.

When I was lost, I felt disconnected within and from all parts of life. I didn't know how to move at all. One day I had a dream that I was crying out for help. An angel came to me and said that if I wanted to be healed fully, I needed to forgive myself for losing my path. I felt such a deep sadness because it was only then that I realized I had separated and lost myself completely. I knew my disconnection was causing me to struggle in my life every day. I woke up with resolve that it was time to connect and heal myself in all aspects of my life. I knew my heart, spirit, and mind needed to be one once again. Even after healing each area through meditation, prayer, energy healing, and consciousness reframing, I still felt like there was something missing. I grew to find that even though I healed, I still rejected my potential self.

Maybe you're struggling with this right now. Maybe you still need to give yourself permission to grow and be free. Maybe at times you feel like you deserve it, but there is some voice still whispering to you that you don't deserve it or that you will never heal.

You have to feel worthy of connecting to your divine being. When you begin to bridge all aspects of your life together, you feel centered and peaceful. You aren't meant to live your life disconnected from your truest self. It can block you from truly living.

As I healed, I felt like I was on a scavenger hunt looking for the missing pieces that had been scattered due to my trauma. But once I started to piece them back together, I started to reclaim my personal power, strength, and freedom. Soon I believed I was worthy of goodness. My heart filled with joy and gladness. I allowed my fullest potential to unfold before my eyes. As we begin to realign with all aspects of our lives, we will become aligned with our truest potential self.

No matter where you are in your healing journey, you have to allow yourself to shift and become connected. You can no longer exist halfway present in your life. We are meant to be whole. I want you to imagine what your full potential looks like. Feel what it's like to accept your being at its highest level.

Ask the question: Who am I meant to be? Now I want you to embody it and embrace it. As you begin to transform yourself, it will create a space where you will feel that you have more vigor to press forward.

We often forget what it would feel like if we were healed completely. We become fixated on our current reality, and we end up losing sight of an eternal perspective in our life. The question shouldn't be, *how am I going to get through this?* It should be, *what does life look like after I have gotten through this?* After we find the answer to this question, we must only focus on the end and allow ourselves to keep trying and give grace if we fail. The purpose is to take action to create and receive this new life we are setting out to reach. Challenge a shift in your perspective that focuses on the joy in your daily life. Allow yourself to embrace a hopeful future.

> **"Transformations can feel exhausting—but that's because you're draining out old energies which no longer serve you, to make room for the new."**
>
> — Vex King

See yourself in your full potential. Focus on it, feel it, and allow it to move you toward love and light. Remember the divine already sees you in your perfection. Your only block is yourself. Spiritual, mental, and physical transformation comes through your prayer and centeredness. You must release the negative energies and then center yourself on the divine. Allow yourself to let go of the pain and sorrow. Keep moving through this pain but shed the trauma and give yourself strength to see your amazing future with each step you take.

∼

Where Can You Find Your Peace?

For the next thirty days meditate and act on how to become in alignment with your potential self.

Spend more time in nature pondering what your future looks like.

Meditate on this question and connect to yourself daily.

19

MENTAL TRANSFORMATION

As you begin to step into your full potential, you need to ensure you have a positive mindset to foster the right environment for your spirit, body, and mind to remain connected. The trauma that caused the disconnect leads to losing hope, happiness, and joy and blocks us from believing that there is light in our life. With part of us disconnected, the darkness seems to rise from within and surround us. It can feel like we are in a box that is constantly closing in on us. We feel stuck and as we seek light, we begin feeling like we are fighting for our lives. But when we allow ourselves to bless and cleanse ourselves from pain, sorrow, anger, and heartache, it will allow us to become free and full of purpose, gratitude, and gladness.

We must seek gladness in our life so we can find a greater sense of purpose in our life daily. Joy allows light, which is how growth in healing takes place. Healing doesn't happen in darkness. Think of joy like the sun and our trauma and negativity are like dark clouds. Whichever we feed will consume the outcome of our day. Just like the sun, our joy will brighten us and will fuel us with the energy to prevail. Joy and gladness will also help you better control your reactions and will allow you to think positively and to form positive patterns that will help you heal and thrive in your life.

In the midst of my healing, I would try to find joy in my life no matter what I was feeling or going through each day. Joy is your soul's advocate that is always pulling you back to that beautiful garden of calmness and centeredness. I actively sought things that would bring me joy when I struggled to keep my head above the water. I urge you to find something that will bring you joy instantly. Maybe you like to draw, dance, or sing. Maybe spending time with others or being out in nature brings you joy. Whatever it is, write it down. Allow this to be the blueprint of what to do whenever you are feeling low and need to brighten up your day.

At times, it's easy to feel like there's nothing else inside, even when you're on your healing journey and have made a lot of progress. Healing is a growth process, and it naturally ebbs and flows. But something that was always comforting to me was that I learned how to be happy even when life was hard. There was a day that I could feel control slipping from my fingers, as it was clear I had no control of the outcome that I faced. The temptation to slip was there, but instead, I chose to instill positivity in a negative reality. I reminded myself that no matter what happens to me, I have what it takes to keep going. So, I searched for what could be my happy place. Something that could bring me joy. For me, it was simply going for a long walk in nature. I felt calm and happy instantly, and it fueled

Healing the Survivors

me with the energy to not slide back in the progress I had made.

When we have joy in our lives, it gives us more bravery and resolve to keep going no matter what the circumstances are. Allow your gladness to help heal you. Choose to seek gratitude each day and reflect on how far you have come. Reflect on where you were and where you are now. Be proud of yourself because you have come a long way. It's not easy, but you're doing it and you need to own the incredible progress. Continue to encourage yourself to show up each day for one more step forward. Become intentional as you wake up each morning. Don't just go through the motions in life. If we are unintentional, we will take our life for granted, and that's when it becomes easier to disconnect from reality again. Our happiness is not something that we find, it is something we become. It is something we embody, and with it, life becomes better and brighter.

"Transformation means to me...reassessing and then taking action on redefining and remodeling me to be the best of my ability."

— Linda Hinds-Alexander

We must strive to find joy every day from here on out. You can no longer be a prisoner to your emotions. Choose freedom and permit yourself to reconnect with your authentic self. Decide to be in the moment and focus on the joy through gladness and gratitude. Be mindful of how you are spending each day. Rest in a constant state of peace and happiness. Choose to be positive and have an eternal perspective on life.

Strive to find joy in the journey of healing and reaching your full potential. It starts with you, and only you can master your joy. Allow your spirit, mind, and body to embrace this joy and have a deep connection with it. Because when chaos arises, joy and gratitude will help you have the strength and power to endure until the end and come out more refined than ever.

∽

Affirmation

I have the power to shape my ideal reality.

I am worthy of stepping into my fullest potential.

I am worthy of feeling happy.

I am worthy of love, happiness, and joy.

20

A PURPOSEFUL TRANSFORMATION

*O*nce you find true happiness and step into your full potential, you must step into a purposeful life. Finding your true purpose will guide you to clarity and direction with your future, like a compass. It will also give you a reason to get up every morning and motivate you when times are hard. As we heal, this is something we need so we can keep fighting every single day.

Your life purpose will guide you to create a meaningful life. When we don't have clarity in our purpose, we feel lost, uncertain, and lack determination to move forward. When we know what our purpose is, it directs us on next steps with every decision we make. It helps us not only survive in life, but create deeper meanings to everything you interact with. Your purpose will energize you and help you get out of bed in the morning. It will inspire you to keep going and prevent you from giving up. When you find your purpose, it will allow you to have a sense of belonging. Having a purpose connects your full potential self to the world around you.

I remember days when I felt uncertain about what that purpose looked like. The vision of it was hazy. But as I meditated and pondered the questions of the things that make me unique and of my full potential, I clearly saw that my purpose drives the peace behind why I was meant to survive and prosper.

Maybe you are still feeling lost and uncertain on what that purpose is. I challenge you to start evaluating your journey, the things that make you happy, and what your fullest potential looks like to help you arrive at an answer. Meditate on it. Sometimes it won't come right away but don't give up on it. When you are ready it will present itself to you.

Your "why" behind everything you do truly matters. It will shape you and create a meaningful life outside of your trauma. When you live a purposeful life, you will live a positive life and start experiencing the world differently. What used to feel dark and foggy will now become bright and airy. As we feel a sense of purpose, we can breathe better. If you are still battling feelings like you don't matter or that you have nothing to live for, finding your purpose in life will allow you to awaken your true self, and it will bring a deeper understanding of why you are needed and meant to lead a prosperous life. You are meant for greater things, and you are meant to overcome your current reality. You are meant for more.

Finding my purpose helped me take longer strides to move forward in my life. I felt a sense of belonging and a bigger understanding of why I was meant to keep going no matter how hard life got. Some days were challenging, but knowing I was meant for something greater than my current reality helped me maintain an eternal perspective. I wanted to not only achieve my purpose, but to become something more than the trauma of my past because that no longer defined me.

> "You have to look deeper, way below the anger, the hurt, the hate, the jealousy, the self-pity, way down deeper where the dreams lie, son. Find your dream. It's the pursuit of the dream that heals you."
>
> — BILLY MILLS

If you desire change and you want to truly heal and overcome your trauma, seek to find your purpose in life. Make it a priority. Once you find it, it will lead you to peace, joy, and happiness. Soon you will unlock your full potential, and you will be reborn with a new perspective and into a positive you.

∽

Finding Your Purpose in Life

What is most important to me?

I feel most alive when...? How do I feel?

How do I want to be remembered fifty years from now?

How can I make the world a better place?

STEP 8
FREEDOM

21

SET GOALS

$\mathcal{A}$s I gathered all my missing puzzle pieces together that I needed to fully heal myself, I reflected on how far I had come and where I am headed. My body and heart were filled with joy and gratitude. In my soul, I knew I was meant for greatness, and I was grateful that it started to unfold before my eyes. I believed I was strong and powerful, and I started to see my true potential reveal itself each day. I felt like a completely new person. I finally was free from my trauma, and I was ready to move forward and become the best version of myself. I was ready to step onto the path of freedom so that I could completely rid myself of the past.

"When you know who you are; when your mission is clear, and you burn with the inner fire of unbreakable will; no cold can touch your heart; no deluge can dampen your purpose. You know that you are alive."

— CHIEF SEATTLE, DUWAMISH

When we are ready to truly move forward in our lives, we need to take the first step of committing to a better life. As we heal, we need to set goals to help us take action to move forward. Without goals, we often fall back into old patterns, sliding back to ground zero. For us to have better results and stay on track of our healing, we need to set meaningful goals to keep us motivated and to help us leave the path that no longer serves us.

Setting goals will help you create a roadmap on how to move forward in your life after overcoming your trauma. Goals can help you take action to become the best version of yourself.

I remember when I made my goals after healing. They consisted of having balance in all aspects of my life. I had goals for my relationships, career, mental health, physical health, and spirituality. By having goals in different areas of my life, I could keep a positive outlook on my entire journey. They kept me motivated because I knew I was constantly progressing. Often in the middle of our trauma, we are stuck feeling motionless, and we forget about the wonderment of dreaming and creating goals. Sometimes we believe that we can't dream anymore. Wherever you are in your healing journey, I want you to know that you are allowed to dream of a life where your trauma no longer controls you. Once you create that dream, I want you to focus on it and accept that this dream will be the only outcome in your life. Then I want you to consider your current reality, what you currently have, what you're currently facing, and what must you do each day to overcome it. That's part one of your roadmap.

As I healed, I learned the importance of re-

Healing the Survivors

flecting on the ways I could better myself, and it helped create a life worth living. I remember one day after an Emotion Code session I had with my practitioner, I decided that I wanted to help survivors heal and empower themselves to step into their full potential selves. At that moment, I created a goal. A goal that I would do whatever was in my power to make sure I achieved it. I decided that I would dedicate my life to inspire and elevate survivors in the midst of their journeys so that they would know that healing was possible. This goal has helped me create a life that I never knew I could have. It forced me to get out of my comfort zone, but it also freed me of my negative beliefs that tried to block a life that I desired and that was truly worth living.

When we create powerful goals, it will propel us forward. It will give us a deeper meaning of life, help us continue to better ourselves daily, and create endless possibilities to make our goals come true. No matter what we are struggling with in our lives, setting goals allows us to dream outside of our trauma, and it becomes the gateway to our freedom and joy.

Before you can create your goals, you need to have a grasp on your current reality. You must understand the areas you want to grow and change so that you can make the proper actions to do so.

To help me create my goals, I wrote about my current reality in each area of my life and scaled them from one to ten. Visually seeing them written down helped me understand the actions I needed to take to improve each area of my life to a higher number. This motivated me to improve myself and my well-being because I knew I had the choice and freedom to create the life that I wanted. As survivors, it is important to keep in mind that we don't have to stay in our current reality forever. We have the freedom to consciously choose a better life, and we have the freedom to strive for it daily.

When we create goals, we need to be specific. We can't have goals that are too general like, "My goal is to be happy." This goal is great, but it doesn't give us a direction on how to become happy nor does it help us accomplish happiness. We must develop SMART goals. SMART goals allow us to create Specific, Measurable, Attainable, Realistic, and Time-based goals. We must create goals that allow us to improve ourselves. When you make goals that are Specific, Measurable, Attainable, Realistic, and Time-based it will increase your odds for success because it will create a roadmap on the steps needed to achieve this goal. Note that these goals can be long-term or short-term. It is up to you to decide.

Allow yourself to dream and invest in yourself so that you can create the life that you deserve. You are worthy of your future, and you are worthy of being successful in all aspects of your life! Now it's time for you to step into it. You can take small steps, or you can leap into your future, but the goals you set and reach will determine the outcome of your life.

So, what will your goals be? Get to writing and start planning your future because you are the only one who can create this new path for yourself.

Exercise

Identify your goals on a spiritual, mental, and physical level.

Create a step-by-step plan on how to achieve your goal daily.

Take the first step and get started.

22

MOVE FORWARD

The art of moving forward is such a rewarding and freeing experience. To me it feels like jumping into cold water on a hot summer day. It's exciting, and it's refreshing, and it feels like all the weight has been lifted off you. It is such a powerful moment in your life, and it will be the beginning of something new and transformational.

The beauty of moving forward is that we get to wipe clean the writing of the past. We get to rewrite our story and include the beautiful and powerful truths about ourselves and what we have endured. We now can embrace the life we are living, and we can accept that there is hope within our freedom. We get the power to choose our destiny, and we are no longer stuck reliving the hell of our past. We decide to close the door on our past and step into a better and brighter room where we truly belong.

Our trauma no longer has control over us. We are set free, and we can now find our way back to our full potential self because there is nothing blocking us from reaching it. As you find your freedom and start to move forward, allow yourself to have closure with your past. To find closure, ask yourself, *am I still holding onto anything preventing me from moving forward?* If so, what does it mean, and what do you need to do to release it so you can take the necessary actions? When we ask ourselves these questions, it will allow us to have closure so that we can truly heal and accept our freedom.

However, give yourself permission to move forward whether you have closure or not. Don't allow it to consume you and block you from moving forward in your life. If you need closure to move forward, write a letter to unleash your thoughts; allow all your emotions to surface whether it is joy, anger, frustration, or confusion. Let it all release from you. Once you are done, seal it up and burn it. Permit the past to burn with it as well. From here on, it will no longer control you, and you will be blessed with the freedom to move forward with your life.

As I was ready to progress from my past, I had a dream that pushed me into the sea of freedom. I was standing in a doorway, waving goodbye to the past and to my old self. I could feel a powerful energy come over me as though I was being blanketed with strength and protection so that I would be safe moving forward on my journey. As I turned, facing the openness of a field, I felt like I was looking toward my future. As I took the first step, I could feel someone lifting me up as they whispered, "From here on out, you will be filled with peace, joy, freedom, and the strength and power to endure until the end wherever your path leads you." I remember as I started walking forward, I was no longer filled with fear, sadness, and hopelessness. Instead I was filled with excitement. I knew I would be safe and that nothing would get in my way of having power over my own life again.

> "The only thing a person can ever really do is keep moving forward. Take that big leap forward without hesitation, without once looking back. Simply forget the past and forge toward the future."
>
> — ALYSON NOEL

Choose at this point to no longer dwell on the past but to move past it. It will not control you again. Learn how to live in the moment where you look ahead and not behind. When we live in the moment, it allows us to stay present and calm no matter what situation is at hand. Choose to focus on the positives in life and begin surrounding yourself with people who will encourage you and embrace you on your journey moving forward. Allow yourself to choose happiness and to accept love and joy into your life each day. Remember that you are in charge of your future, and you have the power to create a better life for yourself. It starts with a choice.

∽

JACQUELYN WEIS

Affirmation for Moving Forward

I am worthy of creating my own destiny.

I move forward fearlessly and excitedly.

I am moving forward with confidence and with ease.

I am worthy of freedom.

23

HEAL OTHERS

"You're not a victim for sharing your story. You are a survivor setting the world on fire with your truth. You never know who needs your light, your warmth and raging courage."

— ALEX ELLE

As we transition into our new beginning, we can become a voice to uplift others. When we share our story, it allows us to take control of our own story. By sharing it with others, it will encourage them so they too can heal. We can't be quiet anymore; we have to advocate for others who are in the beginning of their healing. It's time to take a stand, and by sharing your story, it will empower you as you lead others to safety and light.

I remember when I was sixteen-years-old, and I was working with Native American youth in Portland, Oregon. I shared my survivor story with a room of young girls and encouraged them that they too can heal and reach their full potential. I remember after speaking with them, empowerment, peace, and strength washed over me. I knew in that moment that I was meant to help lead others and support survivors so that they could heal and move forward in life. Later that afternoon, I received several emails about how they were inspired to finally heal. They echoed the hopelessness I felt early in my journey. They believed just like I did that they would have to live the rest of their lives powerless and afraid. One of the girls I had spoken to had dropped out of high school because she had lost all hope after her trauma and had given up on her future. Three months later, she sent me a photo of her holding her GED.

You never know what your story can do for others. We aren't meant to heal others, nor is it our responsibility to do so. But if you are ready to extend a hand, it will be the most inspiring thing you could possibly do in your life. As survivors we are meant to uplift one another. It is time to be the answers to someone's prayers. You never know what someone else is facing until you offer help and embrace them. Become someone else's hope. Become the person you needed when you were healing. Show them that it is possible to heal and that there's so much more than our trauma waiting on the other side of this journey.

We can no longer allow others to do this alone. Join an advocacy group; share your story in your own way. Take action to share your voice and spread the message that there is still hope. Allow your gifts to come forward. Whether you are a writer, artist, poet, or dancer, express yourself and own your story of the past. Through outreach, encouragement, and getting involved in various groups and organizations, help serve others so that they have hope. Your story has power! Use it!

We have the power to make a difference in other survivors' lives. Having your voice shared will bring hope and uplift others as they are seeking for ways to heal and help themselves. Let's not do this alone. We have to empower those who don't feel seen and heard. Too many people are hurting and seeking a sign to keep going. You never know who may be waiting for your story. It can cause a ripple effect in healing this world. Become a voice of truth and strength. Encourage others to heal themselves and become free. Share your story, share what you did to heal, even share this book with them. You will never know the impact you can make until you step outside and seek those who need healing in their life.

Be willing to lead others out of their darkness and allow yourself to become your full potential. When you become your full potential, you will leave an everlasting imprint on yourself and others. Your healing effect on others will last a lifetime. Be proud of your journey and embrace the future, for you hold the keys to your happiness.

∽

Exercise: Becoming Free

Who are you now, and who are you becoming?

What do you want your life to look like five years from now?

What advice would you give yourself at the beginning of your healing journey?

CONCLUSION

As you look toward your future, remember the things you have overcome and allow the strength of healing from your past launch you into your future. Every breath you take from here on will determine your tomorrow so challenge yourself to strive for peace and love each day. Allow forgiveness into your heart, release the burden you carry and freely transform and become the person you are meant to be. Burn the bridges of your past; they no longer define you.

Allow yourself to implement the teachings into your life. Continue to heal and transform yourself. It doesn't end here. I want you to continue searching for your purpose and your full potential.

I encourage you to implement these steps into your daily life and allow them to heal and transform you. If you need help healing, visit my website www.jacquelynweis.com to schedule a healing session with me personally. Continue to look forward; your life is about to transform.

Live each day striving to be better than yesterday. Share your voice and learn to lead others be-

Conclusion

cause with your strength, others will heal. Join the "Healing the Survivors" private Facebook group. Join groups in your communities to allow your voice to be heard and allow your inspirational story to be the voice of others. It's time to fly and become who you were always meant to be.

RESOURCES

Join the Healing the Survivors private Facebook group with Jacquelyn Weis
https://www.facebook.com/groups/healingthesurvivorssupportgroup

The below are U.S.-Based Resources

National Domestic Violence Hotline
1-800-799-7233

National Sexual Assault Hotline
1-800-656-4673
online.rainn.org

Planned Parenthood
1-800-230-7526
www.plannedparenthood.org

StrongHearts Native Helpline
844-762-8483

National Teen Dating Abuse Helpline

Resources

    1-866-331-9474
    www.loveisrespect.org

National Suicide Prevention Lifeline
    1-800-273-8255
    www.suicidepreventionlifeline.org

REFERENCES

Chapter 1
1. Arnold, C. (2018, April 23). Life After Rape: The Sexual Assault Issue No One's Talking About. Women's Health; Women's Health. https://www.womenshealthmag.com/life/a19899018/ptsd-after-rape/

Chapter 4
1. Cornah, D. (2006) The impact of spirituality on mental health [Review of The impact of spirituality on mental health]. Mental Health Foundation. https://www.mentalhealth.org.uk/sites/default/files/impact-spirituality.pdf

Chapter 5
1. Abuse Guardian. (2019, March 13). Abuse Guardian. Abuseguardian.com. https://abuseguardian.com/fight-flight-freeze-the-new-science-of-trauma/

Chapter 6
1. Chevalier, G., Sinatra, S. T., Oschman, J. L.,

References

Sokal, K., & Sokal, P. (2012). Earthing: Health Implications of Reconnecting the Human Body to the Earth's Surface Electrons. Journal of Environmental and Public Health, 2012, 1–8. https://doi.org/10.1155/2012/291541

Chapter 7

1. Lindenfeld, G., & Bruursema, L. R. (n.d.). Resetting the Fear Switch in PTSD: A Novel Treatment Using Acoustical Neuromodulation to Modify Memory Reconsolidation. Www.Academia.Edu. Retrieved October 31, 2020, from https://www.academia.edu/12532059/Resetting_the_Fear_Switch_in_PTSD_A_Novel_Treatment_Using_Acoustical_Neuromodulation_to_Modify_Memory_Reconsolidation

Chapter 10

1. Unwanted memories: How to forget them. (2018, August 14). Www.Medicalnewstoday.Com. https://www.medicalnewstoday.com/articles/251655

Benoit, R. G., & Anderson, M. C. (2012). Opposing Mechanisms Support the Voluntary Forgetting of Unwanted Memories. Neuron, 76(2), 450–460. https://doi.org/10.1016/j.neuron.2012.07.025

Referred Book

Nelson, B. (2019). The Emotion Code : how to release your trapped emotions for abundant health, love, and happiness. St. Martin's Essentials.

ABOUT JACQUELYN WEIS

Jacquelyn Weis is enrolled with the Northwestern Band of Shoshone Nation and lives in Camas, Washington. She is a Certified Emotion Code Practitioner, Body Code Practitioner, T3 Therapist, Native Herbalist, Native Holistic Healer, Author, mother, and wife.

You can follow Jacquelyn at www.JacquelynWeis.com

ACKNOWLEDGMENTS

I would like to thank my amazing family and friends and those who have helped me along in my writing. I would like to thank The InsideOut Institute and Todd Cahill for supporting me through my journey of becoming an author! Special thanks to my amazing publisher Lauren Eckhardt for helping my book come alive.

Most of all I want to thank my husband and soul mate, Tyler Weis for his amazing support, heart, and encouragement.

Finally I would like to say thank you to my readers, I greatly appreciate your support!